British Diabetic

Living with diabetes is not easy! But
and a little reassurance, there's no re
the full.

CW01431899

The British Diabetic Association (BDA) which has been helping people for over 60 years, will probably have the answers to most of your questions and has information on subjects such as hypos, blood glucose testing, holidays and travel, employment and insurance. All members receive *Balance*, the BDA magazine, free every two months keeping them up-to-date with the latest developments.

Talking to people who have been through a similar situation can often be very helpful. The BDA has over 400 local groups and branches throughout the UK which can provide this support and they hold regular meetings and social events too. The BDA is opening regional offices in the UK to help improve the level of local support.

The BDA supports research to improve treatments and to find a prevention or cure for diabetes and its complications. Although dependent on voluntary subscriptions and donations, the Association is the largest single contributor to diabetes research in the UK.

The BDA also represents you – campaigning for improved healthcare services and making representations to the Government on your behalf. Everyone is urged to join the BDA – the larger our membership, the greater our influence on your behalf.

Contact the BDA, 10 Queen Anne Street, London W1M 0BD.
Tel: 071 323 1531.

Registered Charity No. 215199

Other booklets available in this series include:

The Vegetarian and Diabetes
Successful Slimming
Everday Recipes for One and Two
Home Preserves
The Coeliac Condition and Diabetes
Healthy Recipes – Celebrating Sixty Years
Home Baking

All booklets in this series are available from the British Diabetic Association priced at £1.99 including postage and packing. Please use the Order Form at the back of this booklet.

Contents

Introduction

Christmas is the time of year most associated with social gatherings, celebration and parties, all of which can mean changes in your normal routine. Food is a traditional and important part of the festivities, so it is not surprising that many people with diabetes become a little apprehensive as the time approaches.

But Christmas is a time for enjoyment, so try and make everything as normal as possible for both yourself and your family too. With a little care and forward planning you can enjoy the festive season and stay in control of your diabetes.

This booklet contains advice and recipes which will help you make the most of Christmas. The recipes are all based on healthy eating and can be enjoyed by the whole family.

PLANNING AHEAD

A visit to your dietitian may reveal that you can be more flexible with your diet than you thought. If your diabetes is treated with insulin, it may be possible to adjust your dosage and timing to take into account any extra carbohydrate and re-arrangement of meal times. Your doctor or diabetes specialist nurse will be able to teach you how to do this.

To reassure yourself, you can easily keep a check on your diabetes control by testing your blood glucose with a meter or by doing a urine test. Again, your doctor or diabetes specialist nurse will be able to show you how these tests are done.

Remember to eat regular meals - it is better to space meals and snacks throughout the day than to demolish a feast in one sitting. Try cutting down on your carbohydrate at a main meal so that you can have two snacks instead of one. This would enable you to enjoy mince pies and sausage rolls, for example, with everyone else.

PRACTICAL TIPS

1. Try to resist filling up on crisps, nuts and other nibbles before a meal. These can quickly increase your fat and calorie intake without you noticing.

2. If eating out, choose a low calorie starter. Remember that the more starter you eat, the less room you will have for the main course.

3. Pace yourself during a large meal to avoid over-eating or to allow for any in-between meal extras.

4. Take it easy if you are offered a lot of extras.

5. There is no reason why you can't enjoy a small portion of ordinary Christmas pudding or you may like to make one of the recipes in this book which have a reduced sugar content.

6. Similarly, you can enjoy a few sweets and chocolates. As with other goodies, eat them in moderation and spread them throughout the day rather than all at once.

7. Don't be tempted to buy diabetic chocolates and sweets. They are no lower in fat or calories and they are usually very expensive. In addition, some of them can have a laxative effect if eaten in large quantities.

8. Sugar free, reduced sugar, or diet fizzy drinks are useful to keep in the house.

9. And finally, perhaps a brisk stroll in the afternoon will help burn up those extra calories!

ALCOHOL

Your diabetes should not stop you from enjoying a drink unless, of course, you have been advised by your doctor to avoid it for some other reason. However, it does mean that you need to think more carefully about what you drink and when.

As a general rule, everyone (whether you have diabetes or not) should try and keep within the limits of three units of alcohol for men and two units for women in any one day. However, most of us drink more over the Christmas and New Year period than we do at any point during the rest of the year.

Try to have two to three alcohol free days each week. All types of alcoholic drinks have calories so if you are overweight, it is best not to have more than the occasional drink and to count the calories into your daily allowance.

By one unit of alcohol we mean:

Half a pint of beer, lager, or cider
1 standard glass of wine (red, white or rosé)
1 pub measure of spirit (eg vodka, gin)
1 small glass of sherry
1 pub measure of liqueur or aperitif

PRACTICAL GUIDELINES

* Do not substitute alcoholic drinks for your usual meal and never drink on an empty stomach. If you are following a carbohydrate counted diet, alcoholic drinks should not be counted.

* Avoid the low sugar Pilsner type lagers. These tend to have a high alcohol content and so should be treated with caution. Drink the ordinary varieties of beer, lager or cider instead.

* Low alcohol and alcohol free drinks can be useful. If you are driving, make sure that the drink you are taking is alcohol free and not just low alcohol. It is possible to exceed the driving limit with low alcohol drinks if you consume a lot!

* Bear in mind that alcohol free and low alcohol drinks do have a sugar content and so should be treated as a sugary drink. If drunk in moderation, this should not produce a rapid rise in your blood glucose level.

* Always use low calorie mixers with spirits and be careful with home measures as these are often larger than a pub measure! Diluting your drink with plenty of low calorie mixers will make it last longer.

* If you are out for the evening, you could try alternating alcoholic drinks with non-alcoholic ones. Soda water or slimline tonic with ice and lemon can look like a sophisticated drink.

* Sherry or dry wines contain less sugar than the sweet varieties. It is fine to drink up to three sweet wines or sherries (or a mixture of the two) in any one week but try not to drink them all on the same occasion. For example, if you never usually drink but enjoy a sherry on Christmas Day, it really doesn't matter whether it's sweet or dry. If you drink wine regularly, then we would suggest that you stick with the drier varieties.

* Always wear some form of diabetic identification - you and others may confuse a hypo with being drunk. Excess alcohol may also reduce hypo awareness.

Remember:

* Never drink on an empty stomach

* Drink in moderation only

* Never drink and drive

CHRISTMAS HAMPERS

Christmas hampers are often a useful gift idea, and the following list should provide you with a few suggestions. Don't be tempted to include diabetic products as these are not necessary in the diet and are very expensive. The foods listed below are all readily available from major supermarkets and will provide a tasty and healthy hamper.

Useful hamper ideas include:

Canned soups
Canned fish in brine or water
Canned vegetables
Canned kidney beans, chick peas or butter beans
Reduced sugar baked beans
Brown rice
Wholemeal pasta
Packets of high fibre breakfast cereals such as Bran Flakes, Shredded Wheat, Weetabix, unsweetened muesli, porridge oats
Crispbreads or wholemeal crackers
High fibre biscuits such as digestives
Low fat crisps
Reduced calorie salad cream/mayonnaise
Dried fruit
Canned fruit in natural juice
Sugar free jellies
Sugar free dessert whips
Reduced sugar jams or pure fruit spread
Low calorie squash
Low calorie mixer drinks such as lemonade, tonic water or bitter lemon
Alcohol free or dry red/white wine
Fresh fruit and vegetables

CHRISTMAS CAKES

This booklet includes several recipes for reduced sugar rich fruit cakes. These can be successfully used for a Christmas cake. However, due to the reduced sugar content, the cakes cannot be made in advance and stored for weeks as traditional rich fruit cakes can. We suggest that you freeze the cakes if you wish to make them in advance. Defrost and decorate as desired. They should be eaten within 3-4 days. Alternatively, make the cake a few days before Christmas.

There are no suitable alternatives to traditional royal or fondant icing. However, as Christmas is a special occasion (as are birthdays, anniversaries, weddings etc), we would suggest that you decorate the cake in the traditional way. It should not affect your blood glucose level to have a small piece of cake at tea-time, but remember to take account of the extra carbohydrate.

ABOUT THE RECIPES

Each recipe has been calculated to give a total carbohydrate and calorie content. The higher the calorie figure, the more fattening the recipe is! The term 'total CHO' shows the total amount of carbohydrate in the recipe. This is useful if you have been advised to eat a certain amount of carbohydrate foods at certain times throughout the day and will allow you to see how much of the recipe can be fitted into your diet.

Useful Ingredients Measures

WEIGHTS

1 oz/25 g	9 oz/250 g
2 oz/50 g	10 oz/255 g
3 oz/75 g	11 oz/300 g
4 oz/100 g	12 oz/350 g
5 oz/150 g	13 oz/375 g
6 oz/175 g	14 oz/400 g
7 oz/200 g	15 oz/425 g
8 oz/225 g	16 oz/450 g

MEASURING SPOONS

$\frac{1}{2}$ tsp = 1 x 2$\frac{1}{2}$ ml sp
1 tsp = 1 x 5 ml sp
1 dsp = 1 x 10 ml sp
1 tblsp = 1 x 15 ml sp

LIQUID MEASURES

$\frac{1}{4}$ pt = 150 ml
$\frac{1}{2}$ pt = 275 ml
$\frac{3}{4}$ pt = 425 ml
1 pt = 550 ml
2 pt = 1 litre

Useful Dimensions

Diameter for cake tins, flan rings, pie plates

6 inch - 15 cm
7 inch - 18 cm
8 inch - 20 cm
9 inch - 23 cm
10 inch - 26 cm
11 inch - 28 cm
12 inch - 30 $\frac{1}{2}$ cm

Diameters for cutters for scones and biscuits

1 inch - 2$\frac{1}{2}$ cm
2 inch - 5 cm
3 inch - 7$\frac{1}{2}$ cm
4 inch - 10 cm
5 inch - 13 cm

Oven Temperatures

Centigrade	Fahrenheit	Gas
150°	300°	No 2
160°	325°	No 3
180°	350°	No 4
190°	375°	No 5
200°	400°	No 6
220°	425°	No 7
230°	450°	No 8
240°	475°	No 9

Recipes

Starters

MELBA TOAST

Small slices of wholemeal bread. Toast the bread on both sides. Once toasted cut off the crusts and slit the slice in half. Toast the uncooked side.

Serve with soups or pâtés.

GARLIC BREAD

4 oz/100 g low fat spread
2-3 garlic cloves, crushed
2 tblsp/2 x 15 ml sp chopped fresh parsley
2 tblsp/2 x 15 ml sp chopped chives
1 long wholemeal french stick

Total CHO 160 g
Total CALS 1240
Serves 8

Beat together the low fat spread, garlic and herbs until evenly mixed. Slice the french stick at 1 inch (2.5 cm) intervals, taking care not to cut completely through the loaf. Spread each slice on one side with the low fat spread mixture. Wrap in foil and bake in a preheated oven at 200°C/400°F/Gas Mark 6 for 20-25 minutes.

Serve immediately.

Suitable for freezing. Wrap well in foil and freeze for up to two months. Cook from frozen in a preheated oven at 200°C/400°F/Gas Mark 6 for 40-45 minutes.

CHILLED MELON COCKTAIL

These attractive fruit-filled melon halves make a light, refreshing start to a special meal

3 ogen melons
2 medium grapefruits
1 orange
5 oz/125 g frozen raspberries, defrosted and drained
grated rind and juice of 1 lime
a little artificial sweetener (optional)
sprig of fresh mint to garnish

Total CHO Neg
Total CAL 260
Serves 6

Cut the melons in half and discard the seeds. Scoop out a little of the flesh from the centre of each half with a melon baller and place in a bowl. Peel and segment the grapefruits, retaining the juice. Cut the segments in half and place in the bowl, together with the raspberries. Divide the fruit between the melon halves. Sprinkle with a little lime juice and sweetener if used.

Refrigerate and serve chilled.

Not suitable for freezing.

TUNA DIP

7 oz/200 g tin tuna in brine, drained
4 tblsp/4 x 15 ml sp low calorie mayonnaise
3 tblsp/3 x 15ml sp low fat natural yogurt
1 tblsp/1 x 15 ml sp tomato ketchup
1 tblsp/1 x 15 ml sp lemon juice
1 tsp/1 x 5 ml sp Worcestershire sauce
2 spring onions, chopped
freshly ground black pepper
selection of vegetable crudites to serve

Total CHO Neg
Total CALS 430
Serves 4

Place all the ingredients in a bowl and mix well. Season with freshly ground black pepper. Place in a serving dish and chill before serving with a selection of crudites.

Not suitable for freezing.

AUBERGINE DIP

2 small aubergines, (about 1 lb/450 g total weight)
1 onion, finely chopped
2 cloves garlic, crushed
2 tblsp/2 x 15 ml sp low calorie mayonnaise
1 tblsp/1 x 15 ml sp lemon juice
salt and freshly ground pepper
1 tblsp/1 x 15 ml sp chopped coriander
leaves to garnish

Total CHO Neg
Total CALS 180
Serves 4-6

Prick and trim the aubergines. Bake in the oven at 180°C/350°F/Gas Mark 4 for 20 minutes. Leave until cool enough to handle, then peel and chop. Place the aubergine flesh into a blender or food processor with the remaining ingredients and blend until smooth. Place in a serving bowl and sprinkle with the chopped coriander. Serve with vegetable crudites such as mushrooms, carrots, celery, cucumber, cauliflower.

Not suitable for freezing.

TZATZIKI

A refreshing dip, ideal served with vegetable crudites

2 x 5 fl oz/150 g cartons low fat natural yogurt
4 inch/10 cm piece of cucumber, finely diced or grated
1 tblsp/1 x 15 ml sp fresh mint, chopped
1-2 cloves garlic, crushed (optional)
1 sprig fresh mint for garnish

Total CHO 20 g
Total CALS 180
Serves 4-6

Mix together all the ingredients. Chill before serving garnished with the sprig of mint.

Not suitable for freezing.

Note: the CHO value per serving is negligible.

LENTIL PÂTÉ

6 oz/175 g red lentils
1 tblsp/1 x 15 ml sp olive or sunflower oil
1 onion, peeled and chopped
1 clove garlic, crushed
1 tsp/1 x 5 ml sp ground coriander

Total CHO 120 g
Total CALS 880
Serves 12

1 tsp/1 x 5 ml sp ground cumin
½ tsp/1 x 2.5 ml sp turmeric
salt and freshly ground black pepper
2 oz/50g wholemeal breadcrumbs
1 size 3 egg, beaten

Bring the lentils to the boil in plenty of unsalted water. Boil fast for 10 minutes, then cook until tender, drain. Heat the oil and fry the onion and garlic until tender. Add the coriander, cumin, turmeric and seasoning. Stir in the lentils and cook for about 5 minutes on a low heat. Remove from the heat. Stir in the breadcrumbs and egg and place in a lightly greased 1 lb/450g loaf tin.

Cover the tin tightly with lightly greased foil and stand in a roasting tin half filled with hot water. Bake in a pre-heated oven 160°C/325°F/gas Mark 3 for 1-1½ hours or until firm and set. Remove from the roasting tin and leave to cool completely.

Serve sliced.

Not suitable for freezing.

AVOCADO DIP

1 medium ripe avocado
1 small banana, peeled and sliced
5 oz/150 g carton low fat natural yogurt
a few drops of lemon juice

Total CHO 20 g
Total CALS 450
Serves 4-6

Peel the avocado, remove the stone and roughly chop the flesh. Place in a food processor or liquidiser with the remaining ingredients. Blend until smooth. Place in a serving dish, cover and chill until required. Serve with vegetable crudites, small savoury biscuits or slices of pitta bread.

Cook's Tip: Will keep in the refrigerator for up to 2 days. If the dip browns, stir to bring back the colour. If making in advance, keep the avocado stone in the dip to keep the colour.
Remember to remove before serving!

Not suitable for freezing.

HELEN LEE
LYDNEY
GLOS

SMOKED MACKEREL PÂTÉ

8 oz/225 g smoked mackerel fillet, skinned and flaked
7 oz/200 g carton reduced fat soft cheese
dash of tabasco sauce
1-2 tsp/1-2 x 5 ml sp lemon juice
freshly ground black pepper
lemon slices and parsley to garnish

Total CHO Neg*
Total CALS 610
Serves 10

Place all the ingredients in a blender or food processor and process until smooth. Season to taste. Chill until required. Serve spread on small crackers and garnish with a little chopped cucumber, red or green peppers or olives.

Not suitable for freezing.

***Please note:** The amount of carbohydrate for the pate per serving will be negligible. For most small crackers, 5 will give approximately 10 g CHO.

Soups

CARROT AND TOMATO SOUP

2 tblsp/2 x 15 ml sp corn oil
2 onions, peeled and finely chopped
2 lb/900 g carrots, peeled and chopped
2 x 14 oz/2 x 400 g cans tomatoes
2 pints/1 ltr chicken or turkey stock
finely grated rind and juice of 1 orange
salt and freshly ground black pepper
sprig parsley to garnish

Total CHO 80 g
Total CALS 620
Serves 8

Heat the oil in a saucepan, add onion and carrots and cook gently for approximately 5 minutes. Stir in the tomatoes, stock, orange rind and juice and season to taste with salt and pepper. Bring to the boil, stirring, then lower the heat, half cover the lid and simmer for 10-15 minutes until the carrots are tender.

Remove from the heat and leave to cool a little. Purée in an electric blender or work through a sieve until smooth. If the soup is too thick, stir in a little more stock or water. Taste and adjust seasoning. Serve garnished with a sprig of parsley.

Suitable for freezing. Reheat once defrosted over a gentle heat, stirring constantly.

CARROT AND CORIANDER SOUP

1 tblsp/1 x 15 ml sp olive or sunflower oil
1 large onion, chopped
1 lb/450 g carrots, sliced
1 tblsp/1 x 15 ml sp plain flour
1 pt/550 ml chicken or vegetable stock
salt and black pepper
2 tsp/2 x 5 ml sp ground coriander seeds
or 1 tsp/1 x 5 ml sp chopped fresh coriander
1 bay leaf
grated rind and juice of ½ lemon
½ pt/275 ml semi-skimmed milk
chopped fresh coriander to garnish

Total CHO 30 g
Total CALS 420
Serves 4-6

Heat the oil in a large saucepan and gently cook the onion for 5 minutes or until soft. Add the carrots and cook for a further 2-3 minutes. Stir in the flour and cook for a further 1-2 minutes. Gradually stir in the stock, seasoning, coriander, bay leaf and lemon juice.

Bring to the boil, cover and simmer gently for approximately 40 minutes or until the carrots are tender. Discard the bay leaf and purée the soup in a food processor or blender. Return to the pan, add the milk and reheat gently. Adjust the seasoning to taste and serve immediately garnished with chopped coriander.

Suitable for freezing. Freeze after blending. Allow to cool and place in a freezer proof container. Freeze up to 3 months. Defrost thoroughly. Place in a saucepan with the milk and reheat gently. Serve garnished as above.

MUSHROOM SOUP

2 tblsp/2 x 15 ml sp corn or sunflower oil
1 onion, chopped
1 lb/450 g mushrooms, cleaned and chopped
1 tblsp/1 x 15 ml sp plain flour
2 pints/ 1 ltr chicken stock
salt and freshly ground black pepper
pinch of grated nutmeg
1 bay leaf
fresh parsley, chopped
swirl of single or half-fat cream

Total CHO Neg
Total CALS 380
Serves 4-6

Heat the oil in a large pan. Add the onion and mushrooms, cover and cook gently for 5 minutes. Stir in the flour and continue cooking for a further 2 minutes, stirring constantly. Gradually add the chicken stock and bring to the boil, stirring. Add the seasoning. Lower the heat, half-cover, and simmer gently for a further 20 minutes. Purée the soup in a food processor or blender. Adjust seasoning. Before serving, sprinkle with parsley and add a swirl of cream.

Suitable for freezing. Reheat once defrosted over a gentle heat, stirring constantly.

WINTER VEGETABLE SOUP

1 tblsp/1 x 15 ml spoon corn or sunflower oil
1 large onion, peeled and finely chopped
1 clove garlic, crushed
8 oz/225 g swede, peeled and diced
8 oz/225 g carrots, peeled and diced
4 oz/100 g potatoes, peeled and diced
1¾ pints/975 ml vegetable stock
¼ pint/150 ml skimmed milk
salt and freshly ground pepper
chopped fresh parsley to garnish

Total CHO 30 g
Total CALS 410
Serves 4-6

Heat the oil in a large saucepan, add the onion and garlic and fry gently until soft. Add the swede, carrots, potatoes and stock and bring to the boil. Cover and simmer for 25-30 minutes or until the vegetables are soft. Remove from the heat and leave to cool a little. Purée in a blender or food processor to make a smooth purée. Return to the pan, add the milk, check seasoning and reheat.

Serve garnished with parsley.

Suitable for freezing. Reheat once defrosted over a gentle heat, stirring constantly.

Main courses

TURKEY AND RICE RING

Filling:

6 tblsp/6 x 15 ml sp reduced calorie mayonnaise
½ tsp/1 x 2.5 ml sp curry powder
1 oz/ 25 g unsalted cashew nuts
7 oz/200 g cooked turkey, diced
salt and freshly ground black pepper

Total CHO 200 g
Total CALS 940
Serves 10

For the rice ring:

9 oz/250 g brown rice, cooked
7 oz/200 g mixed vegetables, cooked
eg sweetcorn, peppers, peas
2 tblsp/2 x 15 ml sp corn oil
1 tblsp/1 x 15ml sp wine vinegar   } mixed together
¼ tsp/1 x 1.25 ml sp dry mustard
sprinkle of paprika to garnish

Place the mayonnaise and curry powder in a bowl and mix well. Add the cashew nuts and turkey. Stir and season to taste. Chill until required. Place the rice in a large bowl and stir in the chopped vegetables. Add the dressing and toss until coated. Place in a lightly oiled 8 inch (20 cm) ring mould. Chill. Turn out onto a flat serving plate and spoon the turkey mixture into the centre. Sprinkle with a little paprika.

Keep in refrigerator until served.

Not suitable for freezing.

SWEET AND SOUR TURKEY

1 tblsp/1 x 15 ml sp corn or sunflower oil
1 onion, peeled and chopped
1 carrot, peeled and cut into sticks
1 medium sized red pepper, sliced
1 medium sized green pepper, sliced
8 oz/225 g turkey, cooked and diced
4 pineapple rings, canned in natural juice, drained and chopped

Total CHO 50 g
Total CALS 640
Serves 4

8 tblsp/8 x 15 ml sp light soy sauce
3 tblsp/3 x 15 ml sp wine vinegar
1 tblsp/1 x 15 ml sp cornflour
blended with 2 tblsp/2 x 15 ml sp water

Heat the oil in a wok or large frying pan, cook the onion for 2-3 minutes. Add the carrot, peppers and turkey and cook gently for 3-4 minutes, stirring occasionally. Add the pineapple and juice, soy sauce and vinegar and bring to the boil. Stir in the cornflour and water mixture and cook for 2-3 minutes to thicken. Adjust seasoning and serve immediately.

Not suitable for freezing.

TURKEY CURRY

2 tblsp/2 x 15 ml sp corn or sunflower oil
4 turkey breasts, roughly diced
1 large onion, peeled and chopped
2 cloves garlic, crushed
2-3 tblsp/2-3 x 15 ml sp curry powder
1 tblsp/1 x 15 ml sp plain flour
2 tblsp/2 x 15 ml sp tomato purée
juice of ½ lemon
1 oz/25 g desiccated coconut
½ tsp/1 x 2.5 ml sp cinnamon
½ tsp/1 x 2.5 ml sp ground ginger
pinch of cayenne pepper
1 bay leaf
2 tblsp/2 x 15 ml sp mango chutney
salt and freshly ground black pepper
1 pt/550 ml water

Total CHO 20 g
Total CALS 1320
Serves 3-4

Heat the oil in a large saucepan and cook the turkey until browned. Add the onion and garlic and cook for a further 3-4 minutes. Stir in the curry powder, flour, tomato puree, lemon juice and coconut. Mix well. Add the remaining ingredients and bring to the boil, stirring continuously. Reduce the heat, cover and simmer gently for 1-1½ hours or until the turkey is tender, stirring frequently. Serve hot.

Serve with freshly cooked rice.

Suitable for freezing.

Vegetarian

LAYERED PINE NUT ROAST

1 tblsp/1 x 15 ml sp olive or sunflower oil
1 medium onion, finely chopped
4 oz/100 g pine nuts
2 oz/50 g cashew nuts, roughly chopped
2 oz/50 g reduced fat Cheshire or vegetarian cheese, grated
4 oz/100 g fresh wholemeal breadcrumbs
1 tblsp/1 x 15 ml sp fresh chopped parsley
or 1 tsp/1 x 5 ml sp mixed dried herbs
2 size 3 eggs, beaten
a pinch of ground nutmeg
salt and freshly ground black pepper

Total CHO 60 g
Total CALS 1690
Serves 6

Filling:

1 large carrot, peeled and finely diced
1 courgette, finely diced
1 small red pepper, deseeded and finely diced
lemon slices and parsley to garnish

Heat the oil in a saucepan, add the onion and gently cook for 5 minutes until soft and golden brown. Remove from heat, drain and turn into a large bowl. Add the nuts, grated cheese, breadcrumbs, parsley, eggs and seasonings to the onion and mix thoroughly. Quickly stir-fry the vegetables for the filling in the remaining oil until just soft. Place half the nut mixture into a lightly greased and base-lined 2 lb (900 g) loaf tin. Cover with the stir-fry vegetables, pressing down well. Top with the remaining nut mixture, press down well and smooth the surface. Bake in a preheated oven at 180°C/350°F/Gas Mark 4 for 45-60 minutes. Remove from the oven and leave to stand in the tin for 5 minutes. Turn out carefully onto a serving dish. Garnish with lemon slices and parsley. Serve with fresh vegetables, accompanied by Tomato Sauce with Basil if desired. (See recipe on page 23.)

Christmas Cookery

TOMATO SAUCE WITH BASIL

1 x 14 oz/400 g can chopped tomatoes
1-2 cloves garlic, crushed
2 tblsp/2 x 15 ml sp red wine (optional)
2 tblsp/2 x 15 ml sp fresh basil, chopped
salt and freshly ground black pepper

Total CHO Neg
Total CALS 70
Serves 6

Place all the ingredients in a saucepan. Bring to the boil and simmer, uncovered for about 10 minutes until thick, stirring occasionally. Check seasoning and serve hot with the layered pine nut roast.

SPINACH AND LENTIL ROULADE

3 oz/75 g red lentils
1 small onion, chopped
1 tblsp/1 x 15 ml sp tomato purée
½ tsp/ 1 x 2.5 ml sp cumin (optional)
1 lb/450 g frozen spinach, defrosted
1 oz/ 25 g low fat spread
1 oz/25 g wholemeal flour
½ pint/275 ml skimmed milk
2 size 3 eggs, separated

Total CHO 70 g
Total CALS 810
Serves 4-6

Grease and line an 11 inch /28 cm swiss roll tin. Bring the lentils to the boil in plenty of unsalted water. Boil fast for 10 minutes, then drain. Return to the pan, add the onion and cook uncovered until tender. Continue heating to evaporate any excess moisture. Add the tomato purée and cumin (if using), and season to taste. Cook the spinach (do not add any water) for 3-4 minutes. Turn into a colander or sieve and press well to remove as much liquid as possible.

Make the white sauce: place the low fat spread, flour and milk in a saucepan. Whisk continuously over a gentle heat until the sauce thickens. Stir in the spinach and egg yolks and season to taste. Whisk the egg whites and gently fold into the spinach mixture. Spoon into the prepared tin and level the top. Bake for 20-25 minutes at 200°C/400°F/Gas Mark 6 or until golden brown. Turn out onto non stick baking parchment. Spread the lentil purée over the surface and roll up like a swiss roll. Return to the oven for 5-10 minutes. Serve hot.

Not suitable for freezing.

NUT ROAST

1 tblsp/1 x 15 ml corn or sunflower oil
1 onion, finely chopped
8 oz/225 g mixed nuts (peanuts, walnuts,
cashew etc), chopped
4 oz/100 g wholemeal breadcrumbs
(reserve 1 tblsp/1 x 15 ml sp)
¼ pt/150 ml vegetable stock
2 tsp/2 x 5 ml sp yeast extract
a pinch of mixed herbs
salt and freshly ground pepper

Total CHO 50 g
Total CALS 1630
Slices into 12

Heat the oil and cook the onions for 5 minutes or until soft. In a large bowl, combine all the ingredients and mix well. (The mixture should be slack.) Turn onto a lightly greased 1 lb/450 g loaf tin and sprinkle with the remaining breadcrumbs. Bake at 180°C/350°F/Gas 4 for 30 minutes or until golden brown. Allow to cool before turning out. Garnish with sliced tomatoes.

BROCCOLI AND MUSHROOM FLAN

Pastry:

4 oz/100 g wholemeal flour
2 oz/50 g plain flour
a pinch of salt
2 oz/50 g low fat spread
1 oz/25 g white polyunsaturated vegetable fat eg Flora
cold water to bind

Total CHO 140 g
Total CALS 1840
Serves 6-8

Filling:

8 oz/25 g broccoli cut into small florets
4 oz/100 g mushrooms, sliced
1 clove garlic, crushed
4 oz/100 g reduced fat cheddar cheese
2 size 3 eggs, lightly beaten
5 fl oz/142 ml pot half fat single cream
Salt and freshly ground black pepper

Make the pastry - rub the fats into the flour until it resembles fine breadcrumbs. Mix in the water and work to a dough. Chill before rolling out and lining a 10 inch (26 cm) flan ring or dish. Bake blind for 10 minutes at 180°C/350°F/Gas Mark 4.

Meanwhile, steam or boil the broccoli florets until cooked but still crisp. Place them over the base of the pastry case. Add the mushrooms and garlic. Cover with the grated cheese. Beat the eggs with the cream and season to taste. Pour over the flan and bake at 160°C/325°F/Gas Mark 3 for approximately 45 minutes.

Suitable for freezing.

VEGETABLE LASAGNE

Filling:

1 tblsp/1 x 15 ml sp corn or sunflower oil
1 onion, peeled and sliced
1 clove garlic, crushed
1 small green pepper, sliced
2 medium carrots, peeled and thinly sliced
4 oz/100 g button mushrooms, sliced
14 oz/400 g can tomatoes
1 tsp/1 x 5 ml sp mixed herbs
salt and freshly ground black pepper
6 slices wholewheat lasagne or
lasagne verdi

Total CHO 100 g
Total CALS 1080
Serves 4-6

Sauce:

1 oz/25 g polyunsaturated margarine
1 oz/25 g plain flour
½ pt/275 ml skimmed milk
1 oz/25 g reduced fat cheddar cheese

Topping:

1 oz/25 g reduced fat cheddar cheese

Heat the oil in a large saucepan and lightly sauté the onion and garlic until soft. Add the pepper, carrot and mushrooms and cook for approximately 5 minutes. Stir in the tomatoes and season to taste. Allow to simmer for 5-10 minutes, stirring occasionally.

Meanwhile, make the white sauce - place the low fat spread, flour and milk in a saucepan. Whisk continuously over a gentle heat until the sauce thickens. Remove from the heat and stir in the cheese and season to taste. Place vegetable mixture, lasagne and cheese sauce in alternate layers in an oblong 10 x 8 inch (26 x 20 cm) lasagne dish, finishing with the cheese sauce. Sprinkle with the remaining cheese. Cook in a preheated oven at 190°C/375°F/Gas Mark 5 for 40 - 45 minutes.

Party Bites

PRUNE AND BACON ROLLS

20 plump dried ready-to-eat prunes, stoned
20 whole blanched almonds
10 rashers lean back bacon

Total CHO   65 g
Total CALS   750
Makes 20

Fill the cavity of each prune with an almond. Lay the bacon rashers on a board and stretch with the back of a knife. Cut each rasher in half lengthways and wrap around each prune. Place the prune rolls in a foil-lined baking tin and cook under a moderate preheated grill for 5-10 minutes, turning once, until the bacon is crispy. Serve hot, speared with cocktail sticks.

Cook's Tip: To make in advance, make the prune rolls and chill. Grill just before serving.

Not suitable for freezing.

CHEESE AND SPINACH TRIANGLES

1 lb/450 g frozen chopped spinach, thawed
7 oz/200 g reduced fat soft cheese
1 clove garlic, crushed
¼ tsp/1 x 1.25 ml sp grated nutmeg
grated rind of half a lemon
6 sheets filo pastry, thawed if frozen
2 oz/50 g polyunsaturated margarine, melted
salt and freshly ground black pepper.

Total CHO 170 g
Total CALS 1470
Makes approx 24

Cook the spinach in a saucepan over a gentle heat for approximately 10 minutes, stirring occasionally. Press in a sieve to drain off any remaining water and set aside to cool. Place the soft cheese, garlic, nutmeg and grated lemon rind in a bowl. Season to taste. Beat in the spinach and mix thoroughly.

Keep the filo pastry under a damp tea towel while working. Brush one pastry sheet at a time with a little melted fat. Cut each strip lengthways into 3 pieces. Place a heaped teaspoonful of cheese mixture at one end. Fold the pastry over diagonally and keep folding until you reach the end. Continue until all the pastry sheets and filling have been used. Place the triangles on lightly greased baking sheets and brush the tops with the remaining melted fat. Place in a preheated oven and cook at 200°C/400°F Gas Mark 6 for approximately 8-10 minutes or until golden brown.

Serve hot.

Not suitable for freezing.

CHEESE AND HAM TARTLETS

Pastry:

3 oz/75 g plain wholemeal flour
1 oz/25 g plain flour } *sieve together*
a pinch of salt
1 oz/25 g low fat spread
1 oz/25 g white polyunsaturated vegetable fat eg Flora
cold water to mix

Total CHO 70 g
Total CALS 920
Makes approx 12

Filling:

1 size 3 egg, beaten
freshly ground black pepper
3 tblsp/3 x 15 ml sp skimmed milk
2 oz/50 g reduced fat cheddar cheese, grated
2 oz/50 g lean ham, finely diced

Place the flour and salt in a bowl and rub in the fats until the mixture resembles fine breadcrumbs. Add enough cold water to mix to a soft dough. Wrap in greaseproof paper and chill for 30 minutes before rolling. Roll the pastry out onto a lightly floured board and use to line 12 patty tins. Chill.

Meanwhile, prepare the filling. Place the egg in a bowl and season with pepper. Add the milk and cheese and stir well. Place the diced ham in the base of the pastry cases and spoon the egg mixture on top. Cook in a preheated oven at 190°C/375°F/Gas Mark 5 for 10-15 minutes or until golden brown and the filling is set.

Serve hot.

Suitable for freezing.

MARGARET PITT
LIVERPOOL

Christmas Cookery

Starters and Vegetarian Main Meals

Clockwise from top left: Garlic Bread, Mushroom Soup, Lentil Pate and Melba Toast, Vegetable Lasagne, Chilled Melon Cocktail, Spinach and Lentil Roulade, Tsatziki with Vegetable Crudities

Party Bites

Clockwise from top left: *Tuna and Sweetcorn Salad, Salmon and Asparagus Quiche, Ham and Sweetcorn Flan, Red Kidney Beans with Walnuts, Cheese and Spinach Triangles, Waldorf Salad, Sausage Rolls*

Desserts

Clockwise from top left: *Apricot Choux Ring, Gingered Mandarin Gateaux, St Clements Cheesecake, Figgy Christmas Pudding, Celebration Fruit Salad, Trifle, Apple and Mincemeat Jalousie*

Cakes and Pastries

Clockwise from top left: *Mince Pies, Coffee and Walnut Cake, Shortbread, Reduced Sugar Mincemeat, Glazed Christmas Cake, Victoria Sandwich Cake, Dundee Cake*

SALMON AND ASPARAGUS QUICHE

Pastry:

2 oz/50 g plain flour
2 oz/50 g wholemeal self-raising flour
1 oz/25 g white polyunsaturated vegetable fat eg Flora
1 oz/25 g low fat spread
water to bind

Filling:

7 oz/200 g canned salmon in brine, drained
5 asparagus tips
2 eggs
¼ pt/150 ml skimmed milk
salt and freshly ground black pepper

Total CHO 80 g
Total CALS 1200
Serves 6

Rub fat into the flour to make pastry. Add enough water to bind to a soft dough. Roll out thinly to line an 8 inch /20 cm flan dish. Chill for 30 minutes.

Flake and bone the salmon and place in the base of the flan dish. Blanch the asparagus tips in boiling salted water for 5 minutes. Drain and arrange on top of the salmon. Beat the eggs and milk together, add seasoning to taste. Pour over asparagus to fill the pastry case. Bake in a pre-heated oven at 200°C/400°F/Gas Mark 6 for 35-40 minutes. Serve either hot or cold.

Suitable for freezing.

HAM AND SWEETCORN FLAN

Pastry:

4 oz/100 g plain wholemeal flour
2 oz/50 g plain flour
pinch salt
2 oz/50 g low fat spread
1 oz/25 g white polyunsaturated
vegetable fat eg Flora
a little cold water to bind

Total CHO 110 g
Total CALS 1670
Serves 6-8

Filling:

5 oz/150 g sweetcorn
4 oz/100 g lean cooked ham, chopped
4 oz/100 g reduced fat C36heddar cheese, grated
2 size 3 eggs, lightly beaten
¼ pt/150 ml skimmed milk
1 tsp/1 x 5 ml sp dried mixed herbs
salt and freshly ground black pepper

Sieve the flours and salt into a bowl. Rub in the fats until the mixture resembles fine breadcrumbs. Mix in enough water to form a dough and chill in the refrigerator for 30 minutes. Roll out thinly on a lightly floured surface and use to line an 8 inch (20 cm) round or 13 x 4 inch (33 x 10 cm) rectangular flan dish. Bake the pastry case blind for 10 minutes at 180°C/350°F/Gas Mark 4. Remove the paper and beans and cook for a further 5 minutes. Arrange the sweetcorn and ham evenly over the base of the flan case. Cover with the cheese. Beat together the eggs and milk. Add the herbs and season to taste. Pour into the flan case and bake at 190°C/375°F/Gas Mark 5 for 25-30 minutes, until set and golden brown. Serve hot or cold in slices.

Suitable for freezing.

SAUSAGE ROLLS

1 x 12 oz/340 g packet puff pastry   **Total CHO 150 g**
8 oz/225 g reduced fat sausagemeat ⎫ *mix*   **Total Cals 2000**
mixed herbs to taste   ⎭ *together*   **makes 36 bite size rolls**

Roll out the pastry on a lightly floured board. Cut into strips. Roll the sausagemeat into a long sausage and form sausage rolls with the pastry. Brush with egg and milk. Rest in the refrigerator for 10 minutes. Bake at 200°C/400°F/Gas Mark 6 for 15-20 minutes or until golden brown.

Allow to cool on a wire rack.

Suitable for freezing.

MINI PIZZA SNACKS

4 oz/100 g plain wholemeal flour
2 oz/50 g plain flour
a pinch of salt
2 oz/50 g low fat spread
1 oz/25 g white polyunsaturated vegetable fat eg Flora
cold water to bind
8 tsp/8 x 5 ml sp tomato purée
mixed herbs   }   mix
1 oz/25 g Parmesan cheese, grated}   together
2 oz/50g reduced fat Cheddar cheese

Total CHO 120 g
Total CALS 1160
Makes 16

Place the flours and salt in a bowl and rub in the fats until the mixture resembles fine breadcrumbs. Add enough cold water to mix to a soft dough. Chill in the refrigerator for 30 minutes. Roll out and cut out 16 bases using a 2 inch (5 cm) cutter. Use to line a patty tin. Bake blind for 10 minutes. Place 1 tsp/1 x 5 ml sp tomato purée in each case. Sprinkle with herbs and the cheeses. Cook for a further 10-15 minutes at 180°C/350°F/Gas Mark 4. Serve hot or cold.

Suitable for freezing.

TUNA AND SWEETCORN SALAD

12 oz/340 g can sweetcorn, drained
7 oz/200 g can tuna (in brine) drained and flaked
1 carrot, grated
2 sticks celery, finely chopped
1 tblsp/1 x 15 ml sp cider vinegar

Total CHO 40 g
Total CALS 420
Serves 2-3

Mix together all ingredients, adding the vinegar to taste.
Chill before serving.

Not suitable for freezing.

WALDORF SALAD

3 medium red apples
2 tblsp/2 x 15 ml sp lemon juice
2 oz/50 g walnuts, chopped

TOTAL CHO 40 g
TOTAL CALS 640
Serves 4-6

I head celery, chopped
4 tblsp/4 x 15ml sp low fat natural yogurt
Lettuce leaves to garnish

Core the apples and dice, leaving the skin on. Sprinkle with lemon juice to prevent browning. Mix with the nuts, celery mayonnaise and natural yogurt. Arrange the lettuce leaves on a serving dish and place the salad on top. Serve chilled.

COLESLAW

12 oz/350 g white cabbage, finely shredded
4 medium carrots, grated
4 sticks celery, finely chopped
4-6 spring onions, finely chopped (optional)
6 tblsp/6 x 15 ml sp reduced calorie mayonnaise or salad cream
a few snipped chives to garnish

Total CHO 10 g*
Total CALS 440
Serves 8

Place all the vegetables in a large bowl. Add the mayonnaise or salad cream and mix well. Turn into a serving bowl and chill before serving. Garnish with a few chopped chives.

Not suitable for freezing.

***Note:** The carbohydrate per serving will be neglible.

RED KIDNEY BEANS WITH WALNUTS

8 oz/225 g can red kidney beans, drained and rinsed
I small fennel bulb, finely chopped
I onion, peeled and sliced
2 oz/50 g walnuts, chopped
3 tblsp/3 x 15 ml sp olive oil
2-3 tblsp/2-3 x 15 ml sp fresh parsley, chopped
2 cloves garlic, crushed
salt and freshly ground black pepper

Total CHO: 30 g
Total CALS: 800
Serves: 4

Mix the kidney beans, fennel, onion and walnuts together in a salad bowl. Season the olive oil with the parsley, garlic, salt and freshly ground black pepper. Dress the vegetable mixture with it and leave to marinate for an hour or so before serving.

Not suitable for freezing.

Sundries

BREAD SAUCE

1 onion, peeled and quartered
¾ pt/425 ml skimmed or semi-skimmed milk
6 black peppercorns
1 bayleaf
1 blade mace
3 cloves
4 oz/100 g fresh breadcrumbs
a pinch of salt

Total CHO   70 g
Total CALS 440
Serves 6

Place the onion, milk and seasonings in a saucepan and bring to the boil. Remove the pan from the heat, cover tightly and leave to infuse 15 to 20 minutes. Strain and return to the rinsed out pan with the breadcrumbs and salt to taste. Simmer gently to reheat, stirring occasionally. Adjust seasoning before serving.

MUSHROOM AND ONION STUFFING

1 tblsp/1 x 15 ml sp corn or sunflower oil
4 oz/100 g mushrooms, sliced
1 onion, peeled and chopped
4 oz/100 g wholemeal breadcrumbs
1 tblsp/1 x 15 ml sp fresh parsley, chopped
salt and pepper
skimmed milk to bind if necessary

Total CHO 40 g
Total CALS 360
Serves 6-8

Heat the oil in a pan. Add the mushrooms and onion and lightly fry until softened. Transfer to a mixing bowl and stir in remaining ingredients with salt and pepper to taste. Stir well to combine thoroughly. Bind with a little milk if necessary.

Desserts

CHRISTMAS PUDDING

7 oz/200 g wholemeal breadcrumbs
2 oz/50 g dark brown sugar
4 oz/100 g vegetable suet
a pinch of salt
1 tsp/1 x 5 ml sp mixed spice
6 oz/175 g sultanas
6 oz/175 g raisins
4 oz/100 g currants
1 oz/25 g blanched almonds, chopped
1 medium cooking apple, peeled, cored and grated
grated rind and juice of 1 lemon
1 size 3 egg, beaten
¼ pint/150 ml stout, eg Guinness
approximately ⅛ pint/75 ml skimmed milk

Total CHO 465 g
Total CALS 3030
Each pudding will serve 12

Mix together the dry ingredients with the lemon juice, egg and stout. Mix well. Add a little milk if the mixture is too stiff. Place mixture in 2 x 1 pint (550 ml) pyrex bowls which have been lightly oiled. Cover with greaseproof paper and foil. Steam for 2½ - 3½ hours or pressure cook at high pressure for 1½-2 hours (consult manufacturer's guide).

Cover with fresh greaseproof paper and foil for storage.

To serve: reheat by steaming for 2 hours.

Each serving will give approximately 20 g CHO.

FIGGY CHRISTMAS PUDDING

6 oz/150 g dried figs, finely chopped
4 oz/100 g stoned dates, finely chopped
4 oz/100 g currants
4 oz/100 g raisins
4 oz/100 g grated cooking apple (1 medium)
4 oz/100 g finely grated carrot
3 oz/75 g fresh wholemeal breadcrumbs

Total CHO 350 g
Total CALS 1660
Serves 16

1 oz/ 25 g dark muscovado sugar
grated rind and juice of 1 lemon
2 size 2 eggs, beaten
1/4 pt/150 ml skimmed milk
2 tblsp/2 x 15 ml sp brandy or rum
1 tsp/1 x 5 ml sp mixed spice
1 tsp/1 x 5 ml sp ground cinnamon
1/4 tsp/1 x 1.25 ml sp ground mace (optional)

Place all the ingredients in a large bowl and mix together well. (Don't forget to make a wish as you stir!) Cover and leave overnight. Spoon the pudding mixture into a greased and base-lined 2 pt (1 ltr) pudding basin. Press down well, leaving the surface level. Cover with a circle of greaseproof paper and then foil to cover the basin. Tie with string to secure. Steam over a low heat for 3 hours, keeping the water bubbling throughout. Top up with extra boiling water as necessary.

To store: Cool the cooked pudding, remove the foil but leave the original greaseproof paper in place. Cover with fresh foil. Store in a cool dry place for up to three days. Alternatively it may be frozen. Wrap well and freeze for up to three months. Defrost thoroughly before reheating.

To serve: Reheat by steaming for two hours.

APPLE AND MINCEMEAT JALOUSIE

12 oz/350 g packet puff pastry
2 cooking apples, stewed
2 tblsp/2 x 15 ml sp mincemeat
2 tsp/2 x 5 ml sp lemon juice
granulated artificial sweetener to taste
2 tsp/ 2 x 5 ml sp skimmed milk
1 egg white, to glaze

Total CHO 180 g
Total CALS 1480
Serves 12

Cut the pastry in half. Roll out one half to approximately 14 inch x 8 inch (35 cm x 20 cm), and place on a greased baking tray. Add the mincemeat to the apple and lemon juice and sweeten to taste. Spread this mixture over the pastry base, leaving a 1/2 inch border around the edge. Brush the edges with the milk. Roll out remaining half of pastry to same size. Fold in half and cut slits from the fold to the outer edge, leaving a border around the edges. Place on top of apple and unfold to cover the apple completely. Seal around the edges. Glaze with lightly beaten egg white. Bake in a preheated oven at 230°C/450°F/Gas Mark 8 for 25 minutes or until golden brown. Sprinkle with a little artificial sweetener to taste.

Serve hot or cold.

APRICOT CHOUX RING

An alternative dessert for those who dislike Christmas pudding. The choux pastry may be frozen ahead

Pastry:

¼ pt/150 ml water
2 oz/50 g low fat spread
2½ oz/65 g plain flour, sieved
2 size 3 eggs beaten

Total CHO 110 g
Total CALS 980
Serves 6-8

Filling:

7 oz/200 g reduced fat soft cheese
1 x 5 oz/150 g carton diet yogurt, peach or orange flavour
14 oz/400 g can apricot halves in natural juice, drained
and roughly chopped
a little granulated artificial sweetener to serve

Place the water and low fat spread in a saucepan and heat gently until the low fat spread melts. Bring to a rapid boil then remove from the heat. Add the flour all at once and beat hard with a wooden spoon until the mixture leaves the sides of the pan clean. Gradually add the beaten eggs until the mixture is smooth and glossy, leaving a little left for brushing. Pipe or spoon the mixture onto a lightly greased baking sheet to form a 7 inch (18 cm) circle. Brush all over with the remaining beaten egg. Bake in a preheated oven at 220°C/425°F/Gas Mark 7 for 10 minutes. Then reduce the heat and cook at 200°C/400°F/Gas Mark 6 for a further 15-20 minutes. Remove from the oven and slit in half, horizontally. Return both halves to the oven, opened side up for a further 3-4 minutes to dry out the centre. Cool on a cooling rack.

To prepare the filling beat together the soft cheese and yogurt. Add the chopped apricot and mix well. Use to fill the base of the choux ring, then top with the lid. Sprinkle with a little artificial sweetener to serve.

Suitable for freezing. Wrap the unfilled choux ring well after cooling and freeze for up to three months.

Cook's Tip: Ring the changes by using canned peaches, mandarins or fresh fruit for the filling in place of apricots.

GINGERED MANDARIN GATEAUX

4 size 2 eggs
3 oz/75 g castor sugar
4 oz/100 g plain flour
¼ tsp/1 x 1.25 ml sp ground ginger
¼ tsp/1 x 1.25 ml sp mixed spice
1 oz/25 g polyunsaturated margarine, melted and cooled
2 tsp/2 x 5 ml sp caster sugar

Total CHO 200 g
Total CALS 2240
Serves 10

Filling:

½ pt/275 ml whipping cream
1 tblsp/1 x 15 ml sp finely grated fresh root ginger (optional)
2 tblsp/2 x 15 ml sp granulated artificial sweetener
11 oz/300 g can mandarin segments in natural juice, drained
a little granulated artificial sweetener to decorate

Lightly grease a 12 x 10 inches (30 x 25 cm) swiss roll tin and line with greased greaseproof paper. Lightly dredge with a little plain flour. Place the eggs and sugar in the bowl of an electric mixer and whisk on maximum speed until the mixture is thick and the whisk leaves a trail when lifted. (Alternatively, whisk in a bowl over a saucepan of gently simmering water). Sift the flour and spices together twice, and fold lightly and evenly into the egg mixture. Finally, fold in the cooled margarine using a large metal spoon. Pour the mixture into the prepared tin and level the surface. Bake in a preheated oven at 190°C/375°F/Gas Mark 5 for 15-20 minutes, or until pale brown and springy to the touch.

Have a sheet of baking parchment ready, sprinkled with the two teaspoons of sugar. Turn the sponge out onto the paper and peel off the lining paper immediately. Trim the edges of the sponge with a sharp knife. Roll up from the short edge whilst still warm, with the paper inside. Leave to cool completely on a wire rack. Whip the cream until stiff and lightly fold in the ginger and sweetener to taste. Unroll the sponge and remove the paper. Spread three quarters of the cream over the sponge. Reserving 8 of the mandarins for decoration, arrange the remainder over the cream, re-roll the sponge carefully, sprinkle with a little sweetener (optional) and place on a serving dish. Pipe the reserved cream down the centre of the roll and decorate with the remaining mandarins. Chill in the refrigerator until ready to serve.

Not suitable for freezing.

ST CLEMENT'S CHEESECAKE

2 oz/50 g low fat spread
8 digestive biscuits, crushed
7 oz/200 g reduced fat cottage cheese, sieved
7 oz/200 g low fat natural yogurt
grated rind and juice of 1 orange
grated rind and juice of 1 lemon
1 sachet gelatine
3 tblsp/3 x 15 ml sp water
2 size 2 egg whites

Total CHO 110 g
Total CALS 1190
Serves 6

Melt the low fat spread in a saucepan over a gentle heat. Remove from the heat and stir in the biscuit crumbs. Place in the base of an 8 inch / 20 cm flan dish and chill in the refrigerator. Place the sieved cottage cheese in a bowl with the yogurt and mix well. Stir in the grated rind and juice of the lemon and orange. Dissolve the gelatine in the water, following the instructions on the packet. Whisk into the mixture in a steady stream. Whisk the egg whites until stiff and fold into the gelatine mixture. Pour onto the biscuit base and place in the refrigerator until firm. Decorate with fresh fruit in season.

Not suitable for freezing.

TONY CURTIS
GREAT COATES
GRIMSBY

MANDARIN CHEESECAKE

4 oz/100 g low fat spread
8 oz/225 g digestive biscuits, crushed
11 oz/300 g can mandarin segments in natural
juice, drained and juice reserved
7 oz/200 g carton reduced fat soft cheese,
such as Philadelphia Light
4 tblsp/4 x 15 ml sp granulated artificial
sweetener (or to taste)
½ pt/275 ml whipping cream
1 sachet gelatine

Total CHO 200 g
Total CALS 2810
Serves 10

Warm the low fat spread until just melted and stir in the crushed biscuits until evenly mixed. Press in the base of a loose bottomed 9 inch (23 cm) tin and chill in the refrigerator. Reserving a few for decoration, place the remaining mandarins, soft cheese and sweetener in a food processor or blender and process for a few seconds until smooth. Gently heat the reserved mandarin juice, add the gelatine and stir until dissolved. Cool slightly before adding the processed mixture in a thin steady stream. Whip the cream until thick and lightly fold into the mixture. Pour onto the biscuit base and refrigerate until set. Remove from the tin and serve decorated with the reserved mandarins.

Not suitable for freezing.

JANET SOLARI
SHIFNAL
SHROPSHIRE

GLACE FRUIT BOMBE

This dessert makes a delicious and refreshing alternative to Christmas pudding

1 x 0.4 oz/11 g sachet gelatine
2 tblsp/2 x 15 ml sp water
6 oz/170 g can evaporated milk, chilled thoroughly
8 oz/225 g low fat fromage frais
1 tblsp/1 x 15 ml sp granulated artificial sweetener

Total CHO 120 g
Total CALS 830
Serves 6

2 oz/50 g glace cherries, washed and halved
4 oz/100 g seedless raisins, soaked in
2 tblsp/2 x 15 ml sp brandy

Dissolve the gelatine in the water in a bowl set over a pan of gently simmering water. Set aside to cool. Whisk the evaporated milk in a chilled bowl until doubled in size and stiff peaks form. Fold the cooled gelatine into the evaporated milk together with the fromage frais and sweetener. Place in a shallow tray and freeze for 1 hour or until partially set. Turn into a bowl and whisk thoroughly. Beat in the glace cherries and soaked raisins. Place in a lightly greased 2 pt (1 ltr) pudding basin. Freeze overnight or until solid. Remove from the freezer 5 minutes before serving. Turn out onto a serving plate and serve immediately.

TRIFLE

15 oz/411 g can fruit cocktail in natural juice
1 packet sugar free jelly crystals
2 tblsp/2 x 15 ml sp custard powder
½ pt/275 ml skimmed milk
granulated artificial sweetener to taste
5 fl oz/142 ml whipping cream, whipped
1 oz/25 g flaked almonds, toasted

Total CHO 80 g
Total CALS 1090
Serves 6

Drain the fruit and reserve the juice. Place the fruit in the bottom of a serving bowl. Make up the jelly crystals according to the directions on the packet and make up to the 1 pt/550 ml using the reserved juice. Pour the jelly onto the fruit and place in the refrigerator to set. Make up the custard, remove from the heat and sweeten with sweetener to taste. Allow to cool before pouring over the fruit. Top with whipped cream. Chill. Sprinkle with the toasted nuts before serving.

Not suitable for freezing.

BLACKCURRANT FOOL

8 oz/225 g blackcurrants, thawed if frozen
4 oz/100 g virtually fat free plain fromage frais
granulated artificial sweetener to taste
juice of ½ lemon

Total CHO 10 g
Total CALS 110
Serves 4

Decoration

4 tblsp/4 x 15 ml sp virtually fat free plain fromage frais
a few black grapes, halved

Cook the blackcurrants for approximately 10 minutes until tender. Stir in the fromage frais, sweetener and lemon juice. Sieve or process in blender. Pour into 4 dishes and chill in the refrigerator before serving. Place a spoonful of fromage frais on each fool and decorate with a grape half.

Not suitable for freezing.

CELEBRATION FRUIT SALAD

4 oz/100 g black grapes, halved and de-seeded
4 oz/100 g white grapes, halved and de-seeded
2 apples, cored and thinly sliced
2 slices canned pineapple in natural juice,
chopped and juice reserved
1 orange, peeled and segmented
1 tblsp/1 x 15 ml sp lemon juice
1 wine glass dry white wine (optional)

Total CHO 60 g
Total CALS 310
(add 70 calories if
adding wine)
Serves 4

Mix all the fruits together and place in a serving bowl. Pour over the lemon juice, pineapple juice and wine if using. Allow to chill before serving.

Not suitable for freezing.

Pastries and Cakes

REDUCED SUGAR MINCEMEAT

1 medium cooking apple (approx 8 oz/225 g)
peeled, cored and diced
8 oz/225 g currants
8 oz/225 g raisins
8 oz/225 g sultanas
4 oz/100 g glace cherries
4 oz/100 g chopped mixed peel
4 oz/100 g chopped mixed nuts
2 tsp/2 x 5 ml sp mixed spice
grated rind and juice of 1 orange
grated rind and juice of 1 lemon
3-4 fl oz/75-100 ml brandy or rum

Total CHO   570 g
Total CALS 2940
Total per 1oz/25 g =
10 g CHO/170 cals

Place the apple, dried fruit and nuts in a large mixing bowl. Add the spice and stir well. Add the grated rind and juice of the orange and lemon and the alcohol to give a moist mixture. Cover the bowl and leave for 48 hours. Stir well and pack into clean jars. Cover and label as for jam. Store in a refrigerator until required. Use within two weeks. Alternatively, pack into a plastic container and freeze for up to one month.

MRS D M LOCKETT
NEWTON ABBOT

MRS KENDALL'S EASY MINCEMEAT

1 large cooking apple (approximately 6 oz/175 g)
peeled, cored and finely chopped
2 oz/50 g dried dates, finely chopped
2 oz/50 g sultanas
2 oz/50 g low fat spread
4 fl oz/100 ml unsweetened orange juice
½ tsp/1 x 2.5 ml sp cinnamon
½ tsp/1 x 2.5 ml sp mixed spice
pinch of ground cloves

Total CHO   130 g
Total CALS 820

Place all the ingredients in a medium-sized heavy based saucepan. Cook over a gentle heat until the orange juice has been absorbed by the fruit and a wooden spoon can be drawn across the bottom of the pan, leaving a channel for a few seconds (like making chutney). Place in an airtight container. Store in the refrigerator and use within two weeks.

Yields approximately: 12 oz/350 g

Total per 4 oz/100 g = 30 g CHO/90 cals

LATTICE MINCE PIES

Pastry:

8 oz/225 g plain wholemeal flour
3 oz/75 g plain flour
4 oz/100 g low fat spread
2 oz/50 g white polyunsaturated vegetable fat,
eg Flora
cold water to bind

Total CHO 320 g
Total CALS 2520
Makes approx 24
Each mince pie gives approx 10 g CHO

Filling:

24 tsp/24 x 5 ml sp mincemeat a little
milk for glazing
granulated artificial sweetener to taste

Make the pastry and allow to chill in the refrigerator for 30 minutes. Roll out three quarters of the pastry on a lightly floured surface and cut out 24, 2½ inch (6cm) circles. Place in patty tins and place 1 teaspoon of mincemeat into each case. Roll out the remaining pastry and cut into 2½ inch (6cm) wide strips.

Roll over with a little lattice cutter or cut staggered slits in rows with a sharp knife. Open the lattice out. Cut 24, 2½ inch (6cm) circles, wet the edges and place on top of the pies. Seal. Bake in a preheated oven at 200°C/400°F/Gas Mark 6 for 10-15 minutes.

To freeze: Open freeze the uncooked pies in the patty tins until frozen. Remove from the tin and place in layers in freezer-proof containers. Cover, label and freeze for up to three months. To cook: Preheat oven to 200°C/400°F/Gas Mark 6. Place the mince pies into patty tins and brush with a little milk. Cook from frozen for 25-30 minutes. Sprinkle with a little artificial sweetener to serve.

Cook's Tip: I always make my pastry in a food processor which gives a shorter texture and makes handling easier!

MINCE PIES

Pastry:

4 oz/100 g plain wholemeal flour
2 oz/50 g plain flour
2 oz/50 g low fat spread
1 oz/25 g white polyunsaturated vegetable fat eg Flora
cold water to bind

Total CHO 185 g
Total CALS 1260
Makes 12-16

Filling:

12-16 tsp/12-16 x 5 ml sp mincemeat
a little milk for glazing
granulated artificial sweetener

Make the pastry and allow to chill in a refrigerator for 30 minutes. Roll out on a lightly floured board. Using a 2 inch / 5cm cutter and small star cutter, cut out an equal number of bases and stars. Place the pastry circles in patty tins and put 1 tsp/1 x 5ml sp of mincemeat into each. Place a star top on each. Bake at 200°C/400°F/Gas Mark 6. When they come out of the oven, brush with milk and sprinkle with a little sweetener.

Suitable for freezing.

GLAZED CHRISTMAS CAKE

For many families it is customary to have Christmas cake at tea time. This cake is ideal for those who find the traditional marzipan and icing too much after all the festivities!

6 oz/175 g low fat spread
2 oz/50 g soft brown sugar
3 size 3 eggs, beaten
8 oz/225 g wholemeal self-raising flour
a pinch of salt
1 tsp/1 x 5 ml sp mixed spice
1 tblsp/1 x 15 ml sp brandy
7 oz/200 g mixed dried fruit

Total CHO 380 g
Total CALS 2850
Serves 20

Topping:

3 tblsp/3 x 15 ml sp reduced sugar apricot jam, sieved
brazil nuts
walnut halves
glace cherries
few angelica strips

Cream the low fat spread and sugar together until light and fluffy. Add the eggs, one at a time, with a little of the flour. Stir, then beat thoroughly. Stir in the brandy. Beat again. Add the fruit and remaining flour. Fold in lightly. Place the mixture in a lightly greased 7 inch (18cm) round cake tin, double lined with greaseproof paper. Make a small dip in the centre with a metal spoon (to give an evenly cooked surface). Bake for 30 minutes at 180°C/350°F/Gas Mark 4 and for a further 1-1¼ hours at 150°C/300°F/Gas Mark 2 until a skewer when inserted in the centre, comes out clean.

Cool in the tin for 10-15 minutes, then turn onto a wire rack. Gently heat the jam until warm. Brush the top of the cake while still warm with the apricot jam and then decorate attractively with the nuts, glace cherries and angelica. Brush with more jam and leave to cool completely. Store in an airtight container.

Cook's Tip: This cake is best eaten within a few days. Alternatively, it may be frozen before decorating with the glazed topping.

RICH FRUIT CAKE

1 lb/450 g dried fruit such as sultanas,
currants, raisins
2 tblsp/2x15 ml sp dry sherry or brandy
8 oz/225 g dried stoned dates, finely chopped
½ pt/275 ml water
2 oz/50 g mixed chopped nuts
2 tsp/2x 5 ml sp mixed spice
8 oz/225 g plain wholemeal flour
3 tsp/3x 5 ml sp baking powder
finely grated rind of 1 orange
finely grated rind of 1 lemon

Total CHO 580 g
Total CALS 2720
Serves 24

Soak the dried fruit in the sherry or brandy overnight. Place the chopped dates in a pan with the water and cook over a low heat until soft. Mash well and leave to cool. Mix together the soaked fruit, dates and remaining ingredients until thoroughly mixed. Spoon into a lightly greased 8 inch / 20cm round cake tin. Bake in the centre of a preheated oven at 325°C/160°F/Gas Mark 3 for 1½ - 2 hours or until a skewer inserted in the centre comes out clean. Cool on a cooling rack.

Wrap well in foil and store in an airtight tin.

Best eaten within 3-4 days.

Suitable for freezing. Wrap well in foil and freeze for up to one month.

Cook's Tip: Decorate for Christmas with a few nuts and glace cherry halves, glazed with a little warmed reduced sugar apricot jam.

MRS B NEWMAN
SURREY

CELEBRATION CAKE

This is a delicious, moist cake which can be kept for up to two weeks. If you would like to make it further ahead, it is suitable for freezing

5 oz/150 g plain wholemeal flour
½ tsp/1 x 2.5 ml sp salt
1 tsp/1 x 5 ml sp cinnamon
1 tsp/1 x 5 ml sp mixed spice
½ tsp/1 x 2.5 ml sp grated nutmeg

Total CHO 640 g
Total CALS 4650
Serves 32

8 oz/225 g raisins
8 oz/225 g currants
8 oz/225 g sultanas
4 oz/100 g glace cherries, rinsed, dried and quartered
4 oz/100 g flaked almonds
5 oz/150 g polyunsaturated margarine
2 oz/ 50 g soft brown sugar
4 size 3 eggs, beaten
3 tblsp/3 x 15 ml sp brandy
1 tsp/1 x 5 ml sp bicarbonate of soda dissolved in 2 tsp/2 x 5
ml sp warm water
2 tblsp/2 x 15 ml sp additional brandy (optional)

Grease and line an 8 inch (20 cm) round or 7 inch (17.5 cm) square cake tin with a double thickness of greaseproof paper. Tie a double thickness of newspaper around the side of the cake tin to prevent the outside edge of the cake becoming too dry.

Sift together the flour and spices, tipping any bran remaining in the sieve back into the bowl. Mix together the fruit and nuts. Cream the margarine and sugar together until pale and creamy. Gradually beat in the eggs, adding a tablespoon of flour with each egg. Fold in the remaining flour, fruit, brandy and bicarbonate of soda mixture. Spoon the mixture into the prepared tin and level the surface. Make a slight dip in the centre with the back of a spoon. Place in a preheated oven at 150°C/300°F/ Gas Mark 2 for approximately 2½ hours or until a skewer when inserted comes out clean. Cover the cake with several thickenings of newspaper if it starts to become too brown. Allow the cake to cool in the tin for 30 minutes. Turn out onto a wire rack, remove the paper and allow to cool completely. Wrap in greaseproof paper and foil and store in an airtight container.

Best eaten within two weeks.

Cook's Tip: Halfway through the storage the cake may be unwrapped and the base pricked several with a skewer. Drizzle 2 tablespoons of brandy over the base. Re-wrap.

Suitable for freezing.

Decoration: The cake may be decorated for special occasions in the traditional way using marzipan and fondant or royal icing (remember to add the extra carbohydrate to the total for the cake). For birthdays, anniversaries etc there is no reason why a person with diabetes should not enjoy a small piece of cake along with everyone else. This may be eaten at the end of a high fibre meal or included as a snack.

DUNDEE CAKE

6 oz/175 g low fat spread
2 oz/ 50 g caster sugar
3 size 3 eggs, beaten
8 oz/225 g fine self-raising
wholemeal flour
pinch of salt
} *Sieve together (retaining the grain)*

1 tsp/1 x 5 ml sp mixed spice
1 tblsp/1 x 15 ml sp skimmed milk
7 oz/200 g mixed fruit
1 oz/25 g split almonds for decoration

Total CHO 340 g
Total CALS 2520
Serves 16

Cream the low fat spread and sugar until pale and creamy. Add the eggs one at a time, with a little flour. Stir in the milk and mix well. Add the fruit and remaining flour and fold in lightly. Place the mixture in a greased and lined 7 inch (18cm) round cake tin and level the surface. Arrange the split almonds on top in an attractive pattern. Bake in a preheated oven for 1 hour at 180°C/350°F/Gas Mark 4 or until a skewer when inserted comes out clean. Cool on a wire rack. Wrap well and store in an airtight container.

Best eaten within 1-2 days.

Suitable for freezing.

VICTORIA SANDWICH CAKE

6 oz/175 g low fat spread
3 oz/ 75 g caster sugar
3 size 3 eggs, lightly beaten
4 oz/100 g fine self-raising wholemeal flour
3 oz/75 g self-raising flour
½ tsp/1 x 2.5 ml sp baking powder
few drops vanilla essence
2 tblsp/2 x 15 ml sp hot water

Total CHO 200 g
Total CALS 1800
Serves 8-10

Cream the low fat spread and sugar until pale and creamy. Add the eggs a little at a time, beating well after each addition. Lightly fold in half the flour using a metal spoon, then carefully fold in the remainder with the vanilla essence and water. Divide the mixture between two lightly greased and base-lined 7 inch (18cm) sandwich tins. Bake at 190°C/375°F/Gas Mark 5 in the centre of the oven for approximately 20-25 minutes or until golden and firm to the touch. Turn out and cool on a wire rack.

Store in an airtight container.

Best eaten within 2-3 days.

Suitable for freezing.

Cook's Tip: If using pure fruit spread or reduced sugar jam to fill the cake, remember to add the extra carbohydrate and calories. A pretty finishing touch is to sift a little granulated artificial sweetener over a paper doily on top of the cake. When the doily is lifted it will leave a lacy pattern.

Note: We have used a half and half mixture of wholemeal and ordinary flour. However, for this type of recipe you may prefer to use all white flour. As long as your general diet is high in fibre, an occasional piece of cake made with white flour is perfectly acceptable.

COFFEE AND WALNUT CAKE

6 oz/175 g low fat spread
3 oz/75 g caster sugar
3 size 3 eggs, lightly beaten
6 oz/175 g self-raising wholemeal flour
1 tblsp/1 x 15 ml sp coffee concentrate **or**
2tsp/2 x 5 ml sp instant coffee dissolved in 1tblsp/1 x 15 ml sp hot water

Total CHO 210 g
Total CALS 2020
Cuts into 10-12

Topping:

2 oz/50 g low fat spread
4 tblsp/4 x 15 ml sp granulated artificial sweetener
1 tblsp/1 x 15 ml sp coffee concentrate **or**
1tsp/2 x 5 ml sp instant coffee dissolved in 1tsp/1 x 5 ml sp hot water
a few walnut halves for decoration

Cream the low fat spread and sugar until pale in colour. Add the eggs a little at a time, beating well after each addition. Lightly fold in half the flour using a metal spoon, then carefully fold in the rest. Divide the mixture between two lightly greased 7 inch (18cm) sandwich tins. Bake at 190°C/375°F/Gas Mark 5 in the centre of the oven for approximately 20-25 minutes or until golden and firm to the touch. Allow to cool before sandwiching together. Make the icing shortly before use - beat the ingredients together to a smooth paste. Use to decorate the cake. Add a few walnut halves for decoration.

Suitable for freezing

MARZIPAN

(sufficient for top & sides of 7 inch / 18cm cake)

4 oz/100 g ground almonds   **Total CHO 85 g**
2 oz/50 g caster sugar   **Total CALS 1060**
1 oz/25 g plain white flour
1 size 3 eggs

Beat all the ingredients together to form a smooth paste. This can be done by hand or in a food processor. Divide into two and roll out.

SHORTBREAD

This makes an ideal gift

5 oz/150 g polyunsaturated margarine   **Total CHO 170 g**
4 oz/100 g plain flour   **Total CALS 1840**
3 oz/ 75 g self-raising fine wholemeal flour   **Serves 8**
1½ oz/40 g caster sugar

Rub the margarine into the flours until the mixture resembles fine breadcrumbs. Stir in the sugar and knead together until a soft dough is formed, leaving the bowl clean. Press into an 8 inch (20 cm) tin and smooth the top. Flute the edges and prick all over with a fork. Mark into 8 portions. Bake in a preheated oven at 150°C/300°F/Gas Mark 2 for 50-60 minutes. Leave in the tin for 10 minutes before cooling completely on a wire rack.

Wrap in foil and store in an airtight container.

Best eaten within 2-3 days

Not suitable for freezing

Cook's Tip: Sprinkle with a little granulated artificial sweetener if desired.

Drinks

SANGRIA

1 bottle (70 cl) dry red wine
¾ pt/425 ml unsweetened orange juice
2.2 pt / 1 ltr bottle low calorie lemonade
few slices orange
ice

Total CHO 60 g
Total CALS 700
Serves 10

Mix the ingredients together in a large jug or punch bowl. Add the fruit and ice.

Serve chilled.

HOT FRUITY PUNCH

3 apples (cut into 8)
3 oranges (cut into 8)
1 orange cut into thin slices for decoration
12 whole cloves
2 cinnamon sticks
2 bottles red wine
1 pt/550 ml dry sherry
1 pt/550 ml apple juice (unsweetened)

Total CHO 120 g
Total CALS 2140
Serves 12

Place the cut apples and oranges into a large pan with the cinnamon sticks and cloves and pour over the red wine. Bring the contents of the pan to boil and simmer, covered, for 10 minutes. Remove from the heat and leave to infuse for 10 minutes. Strain the wine and discard the solids. Return the wine to the pan, pour in the apple juice and sherry and heat until the liquid starts to bubble at the edges of the pan. Pour into a warm serving bowl and decorate with the orange slices.

Serve immediately.

CHILDREN'S PARTY PUNCH

2 pts/1 ltr low calorie orangeade
2 pts/1 ltr low calorie lemonade
1 pt/550 ml sparkling mineral water
few slices orange/apple
few slices lemon
ice

Total CHO neg
Total CALS neg
Serves 15

Mix the orangeade, lemonade and water together in a large jug or bowl. Add the sliced fruit and ice.

Serve chilled

Index

Order Form

All the cookbooks in this series
are priced at £1.99 each
including package and postage.

	Number Required	Cost
The Vegetarian and Diabetes		
Successful Slimming		
Everyday Recipes for One and Two		
Home Preserves		
The Coeliac Condition and Diabetes		
Healthy Recipes – Celebrating 60 Years		
Home Baking		
Christmas Cookery		
TOTAL		

I enclose £ ....

Donation £ ....

Please make cheque or postal order payable to British Diabetic Association

(BLOCK CAPITALS PLEASE)

Name _____

Address _____

_____

_____

Please complete both sides of this form.

Cut out this form and send it with your remittance to:

British Diabetic Association
10 Queen Anne Street
London
W1M 0BD

Tel: 071 323 1531

Registered Charity No 215199

Please allow three weeks for delivery

Orders may also be made on ordinary note paper

Membership Forms and further information about the
British Diabetic Association can also be obtained from this address.